EXPERIENCE VIETNAM: A TRAVEL PREPARATION GUIDE

DELZY HAMPTON

TABLE OF CONTENT

*What to wear for every season in Vietnam
*Helpful vietnamese phrases
*Safety and security
*Great itineraries

CHAPTER ONE

THE VIETNAMESE EXPERIENCE

The Vietnamese experience is one of great cultural richness and diversity, as well as a history marked by struggles and triumphs. From the ancient kingdoms of Vietnam to the modern day socialist republic, the Vietnamese people have a rich cultural heritage that has been shaped by centuries of invasions, wars, and cultural exchange.

Vietnam has a long history of resistance against foreign rule, dating back to the 10th century when the country was ruled by a series of dynasties and empires. In the 19th century, Vietnam came under the control of France, and was later divided into North and South by the Geneva Accords in 1954. The country was then reunited in 1975 after the fall of South Vietnam and the end of the Vietnam War.

The war had a profound impact on the country, as well as its people. Millions of Vietnamese citizens were displaced, injured, or killed, and the country was left devastated by the conflict. The government was tasked with rebuilding the country and addressing the aftermath of the war, and it has made significant progress in recent decades, including reducing poverty and improving the standard of living for its citizens.

Vietnam is a country of great natural beauty, with lush forests, rolling hills, and pristine beaches. The country is also known for its rich cuisine, with a wide variety of traditional dishes, including pho (a noodle soup), banh mi (a sandwich), and spring rolls. The country is also famous for its traditional art forms, such as silk weaving, pottery, and calligraphy.

The Vietnamese people are a proud and resilient people, who have faced numerous challenges throughout their history. Despite the difficulties they have faced, they remain optimistic and have a strong sense of national pride. Family is highly valued in Vietnamese culture, and the country has a rich tradition of ancestor worship and respect for elders.

Religion also plays an important role in Vietnamese life, with a majority of the population following Buddhism, along with Catholicism, Taoism, and other indigenous beliefs. The country is also home to a number of cultural festivals, such as the Mid-Autumn Festival, the Lunar New Year, and the Hoi An Lantern Festival, which are celebrated with great enthusiasm and joy.

The Vietnamese economy has undergone significant growth and development in recent years, and the country has become a major player in the global economy. The country is a major producer of rice, coffee, and other agricultural products, and is also home to a thriving tourism industry.

In recent years, the country has also become increasingly integrated into the global community, with a growing number of international business and trade partnerships. This has brought new opportunities and challenges to the country, and the government is working to ensure that its citizens benefit from this growth and progress.

The Vietnamese experience is one of a proud and resilient people, with a rich cultural heritage and a bright future. Despite the many challenges they have faced, the Vietnamese people have remained optimistic and have worked tirelessly to build a better future for themselves and their country.

WHAT TO EAT AND DRINK IN VIETNAM

Vietnamese cuisine is a vibrant and diverse blend of flavours, aromas, and ingredients that has been influenced by various cultures over the centuries. The food in Vietnam is widely regarded as some of the best in Southeast Asia and is a must-try for any traveller visiting the country. I'll be exploring the various dishes and drinks that are popular in Vietnam and what you can expect when dining in this beautiful country.

Starting with breakfast, a traditional Vietnamese meal typically consists of rice porridge (cháo), served with various sides such as fried dough sticks (quẩy), pickled vegetables (dưa), and savoury sauces. Another popular breakfast dish is banh mi, a sandwich made with a baguette filled with ingredients such as pork, pâté, cucumber, cilantro, and pickled carrots and daikon.

For lunch and dinner, rice is the staple food in Vietnam, and it is usually served with a variety of meats, vegetables, and sauces. One of the most popular dishes in Vietnam is pho, a noodle soup made with rice noodles and either beef or chicken, flavoured with spices and herbs such as star anise, cinnamon, and cilantro. Other popular dishes include bun cha, a dish of grilled pork served with vermicelli noodles, and bún riêu, a crab soup made with tomatoes and vermicelli noodles.

When it comes to street food, Vietnam has a wealth of delicious and inexpensive options to choose from. Some popular street food dishes include bánh xèo, a savoury pancake filled with shrimp and bean sprouts, and nem rán, fried spring rolls filled with meat and vegetables. Another popular street food snack is gỏi cuốn, fresh spring rolls made with rice paper and filled with ingredients such as pork, shrimp, and vegetables.

For those who love seafood, Vietnam has an abundance of fresh and delicious options to choose from. Some popular seafood dishes include cua rang me, stir-fried crab with lemongrass and chilli, and bánh hỏi tôm, steamed cakes made with shrimp and served with a spicy dipping sauce.

Vietnamese cuisine is also known for its use of herbs and spices, which add depth and flavour to many dishes. Some common herbs used in Vietnamese cooking include cilantro, mint, basil, and lemongrass. In addition to herbs, spices such as chilli, garlic, and ginger are also used to add heat and flavour to dishes.

When it comes to drinks, Vietnam has a number of delicious options to choose from. One of the most popular drinks in Vietnam is iced coffee (cà phê đá), which is made with a strong blend of coffee and sweetened with condensed milk. Another popular drink is sugarcane juice (nước mía), a sweet and refreshing drink made from pressed sugarcane. For those who prefer something a little stronger, rice wine (ruou), is a traditional alcoholic beverage made from fermented rice and is often used in cooking and for special occasions.

Vietnamese cuisine is a diverse and delicious blend of flavours, aromas, and ingredients, and is a must-try for any traveller visiting the country. Whether you're looking for a traditional breakfast, street food, seafood, or drinks, Vietnam has something to offer for everyone. So, be sure to sample as many dishes as you can and enjoy the rich and flavorful food of Vietnam.

WHAT TO BUY IN VIETNAM

Vietnam is also famous for its many shopping opportunities. With its growing economy and increasing tourist numbers, there are many interesting and unique items to buy in Vietnam. Whether you're looking for souvenirs, gifts, or just want to treat yourself to something special, there are plenty of options to choose from.

1. Traditional Crafts

Vietnamese traditional crafts are an excellent way to bring home a piece of the country's rich cultural heritage. Handmade paper lanterns, silk paintings, lacquerware, and pottery are all popular options that can be found throughout the country. These traditional crafts are not only beautiful, but also functional and make great gifts for family and friends.

2. Hand-Embroidered Linens

Vietnam is famous for its hand-embroidered linens, which are available in a wide range of colours and designs. Whether you're looking for tablecloths, napkins, or bedding, there are plenty of options to choose from. These linens are made using traditional techniques passed down from generation to generation and are of the highest quality.

3. Textiles

Vietnamese textiles are some of the best in the world, and there is a great selection of fabrics, scarves, and clothing available in the country. From traditional Ao Dai dresses to modern fashion pieces, there is something for everyone. The quality of the textiles is excellent, and the prices are very reasonable, making it a great place to buy clothing and accessories.

4. Jewellery

Vietnamese jewellery is unique, and there is a wide range of pieces available, from traditional silver and gold jewellery to more contemporary pieces. There are also a number of markets and shops that specialise in jewellery, making it easy to find exactly what you're looking for. Whether you're looking for a special piece for yourself or a gift for someone else, you're sure to find something you'll love.

5. Bamboo Products

Bamboo is a versatile and sustainable material, and there is a great selection of bamboo products available in Vietnam. From baskets and boxes to furniture and home decor, there are plenty of options to choose from. These products are not only environmentally friendly, but also functional and beautiful, making them a great choice for anyone looking to add a touch of nature to their home.

6. Conical Hats

Vietnamese conical hats, also known as "non la," are an iconic part of the country's culture and make great souvenirs. These hats are made from bamboo or palm leaves and are available in a range of colours and designs. They are also very practical and can be used to protect from the sun or rain, making them a great choice for anyone visiting the country.

7. Food and Spices

Vietnamese cuisine is famous for its fresh ingredients, vibrant flavours, and diverse dishes, and there are many food and spice products available to take home. From traditional spices and sauces to dried fruit and coffee, there is something for everyone. These products make great gifts for food lovers or can be used to recreate your favourite Vietnamese dishes at home.

8. Handbags and Accessories

Vietnamese handbags and accessories are both stylish and affordable, making them a great choice for anyone looking to update their wardrobe. From traditional woven baskets to modern leather bags, there is something for everyone. The quality of these products is excellent, and the prices are very reasonable, making it a great place to buy a new accessory or handbag.

Vietnam is a great place to buy a wide range of products, from traditional crafts and textiles to food and spices.

LOCAL MARKET RECOMMENDATIONS

Vietnam is known for its rich culture and diverse economy, and this is reflected in the local markets found throughout the country. The local markets in Vietnam play a crucial role in the economy as they provide a platform for small-scale traders to sell their products and for customers to purchase goods at affordable prices. The local markets are a hub of activity, where people from all walks of life gather to buy and sell goods, exchange ideas and gossip, and engage in social interactions.

There are various types of local markets in Vietnam, ranging from street markets, open-air markets, night markets, and indoor markets. We will explore the different types of local markets in Vietnam and their significance in the local economy.

Street Markets

Street markets are the most common type of local market in Vietnam and are found in almost every town and city. Street markets are often set up on the sidewalks, and vendors sell their goods from small stalls or carts. The street markets offer a wide range of products, including fresh produce, clothing, electronics, and household items. These markets are usually open from early morning until late in the evening and are crowded with people bargaining for the best prices.

Street markets are popular among local residents as they offer a convenient and affordable way to purchase goods. The vendors at the street markets offer a wide range of products, including fresh produce, clothing, electronics, and household items, at prices that are significantly lower than those found in supermarkets and department stores. The street markets also provide an opportunity for local residents to support small-scale traders and the local economy.

Open-air Markets

Open-air markets are a type of local market that is found in many towns and cities throughout Vietnam. These markets are usually set up in a large open area, and vendors sell their goods from stalls or tents. The open-air markets offer a wide range of products, including fresh produce, clothing, electronics, and household items. These markets are usually open from early morning until late in the evening, and they attract large crowds of people from the surrounding areas.

Open-air markets are a popular destination for tourists as they offer a unique cultural experience and a chance to see local life in action. These markets are also a great place to purchase souvenirs, as vendors offer a wide range of products, including traditional clothing, accessories, and handmade crafts. Open-air markets are a significant part of the local economy, as they provide a platform for small-scale traders to sell their products and generate income.

Night Markets

Night markets are a type of local market that is found in many towns and cities throughout Vietnam. These markets are usually set up in the evenings and offer a wide range of products, including fresh produce, clothing, electronics, and household items. The night markets are popular among local residents as they provide a convenient way to purchase goods after work or school. The vendors at the night markets offer products at discounted prices, and the atmosphere is lively and festive.

Night markets are a popular destination for tourists as they offer a unique cultural experience and a chance to see local life in action. These markets are also a great place to try street food, as vendors offer a wide range of traditional dishes and snacks. Night markets play a significant role in the local economy, as they provide a platform for small-scale traders to sell their products and generate income.

Indoor Markets

Indoor markets are a type of local market that is found in many towns and cities throughout Vietnam. These markets are usually located in large buildings and offer a wide range of products, including fresh produce, clothing, electronics, and household items. The indoor markets are air-conditioned and provide a comfortable shopping experience for customers. The vendors at the indoor markets offer products at competitive prices, and the atmosphere is often more organised and less chaotic than in other types of local markets.

Indoor markets are popular among local residents who are looking for a more convenient and organised shopping experience. These markets are also a great destination for tourists who are looking to purchase high-quality goods at affordable prices. Indoor markets play a significant role in the local economy, as they provide a platform for small-scale traders to sell their products and generate income.

BEST MUSEUMS IN VIETNAM

There are many excellent museums in Vietnam, each with its own unique focus and collection, so it can be difficult to choose just a few to visit. However, the following are considered to be some of the best museums in Vietnam, and are well worth a visit for anyone interested in the country's history, culture, and art.

1. Museum of Ethnology - Hanoi

The Museum of Ethnology in Hanoi is one of the most popular museums in Vietnam and is dedicated to the study and preservation of the country's 54 ethnic minority groups. It has a vast collection of artifacts, photographs, and documents that tell the story of each ethnic group and their way of life. The museum also has a large outdoor exhibit area, where visitors can see traditional houses and other structures from different ethnic groups. The museum provides a fascinating glimpse into the diversity of Vietnamese culture, and is a must-visit for anyone interested in the country's history and culture.

2. Ho Chi Minh Museum - Hanoi

The Ho Chi Minh Museum in Hanoi is dedicated to the life and legacy of one of Vietnam's most famous and revered leaders, Ho Chi Minh. The museum showcases the life of Ho Chi Minh, from his early years as a revolutionary, to his role as the country's first president, and his legacy as a national hero. The museum has a vast collection of artifacts and documents related to Ho Chi Minh's life and work, as well as interactive exhibits and multimedia presentations that provide a deeper understanding of this important historical figure.

3. Vietnam Military History Museum - Hanoi

The Vietnam Military History Museum in Hanoi is dedicated to the country's military history, from ancient times to the modern era. The museum has a vast collection of weapons, equipment, and other artifacts from Vietnam's military history, as well as exhibits and displays that provide a comprehensive overview of the country's military heritage. Visitors to the museum can learn about the country's military history, from the earliest battles and wars, to the more recent conflicts and the eventual reunification of North and South Vietnam.

4. Museum of Fine Arts - Hanoi

The Museum of Fine Arts in Hanoi is one of the city's most important cultural institutions, and is dedicated to the preservation and promotion of Vietnamese art and culture. The museum has a large collection of artifacts and works of art, ranging from ancient ceramics and sculptures to contemporary paintings and installations. The museum also has a number of exhibitions and events throughout the year, showcasing the work of

Vietnamese artists and highlighting the country's rich cultural heritage.

5. Ho Chi Minh City Museum - Ho Chi Minh City

The Ho Chi Minh City Museum in Ho Chi Minh City is one of the city's most important cultural institutions, and is dedicated to the history and culture of Ho Chi Minh City and the surrounding region. The museum has a large collection of artifacts, documents, and photographs that tell the story of the city's history, from its early days as a small trading post to its role as a major centre of commerce and culture in modern-day Vietnam. Visitors to the museum can learn about the city's rich cultural heritage, and the events and people that have shaped its history and development.

6. War Remnants Museum - Ho Chi Minh City

The War Remnants Museum in Ho Chi Minh City is a powerful and thought-provoking institution that tells the story of the Vietnam War, and its impact on the country and its people. The museum has a vast collection of artifacts, documents, and photographs that provide a comprehensive overview of the conflict, from its causes to its aftermath. The museum also has a number of exhibits and displays that highlight the human toll of the war, including the impact on civilians, soldiers, and the environment. Despite its sombre subject matter, the War Remnants Museum is an important and educational institution that provides visitors with a deeper understanding of one of the most significant events in Vietnamese history.

7. Museum of Ho Chi Minh City - Ho Chi Minh City

The Museum of Ho Chi Minh City is a comprehensive museum dedicated to the history and culture of the city and its people. The museum has a large collection of artifacts, documents, and photographs that tell the story of Ho Chi Minh City's rich cultural heritage, as well as exhibitions and displays that highlight the city's cultural, economic, and political development. Visitors to the museum can learn about the city's history and its role in shaping the cultural and economic landscape of modern-day Vietnam.

8. Museum of Vietnamese History - Ho Chi Minh City

The Museum of Vietnamese History in Ho Chi Minh City is one of the city's most important cultural institutions, and is dedicated to the preservation and promotion of Vietnamese history and culture. The museum has a vast collection of artifacts, documents, and works of art that span thousands of years of Vietnamese history, from the earliest civilizations to the modern era. The museum also has a number of exhibitions and events throughout the year, showcasing the work of Vietnamese artists and highlighting the country's rich cultural heritage.

9. Museum of the Revolution - Ho Chi Minh City

The Museum of the Revolution in Ho Chi Minh City is a comprehensive museum dedicated to the history of the Vietnamese Revolution, and its impact on the country and its people. The museum has a vast collection of artifacts, documents, and photographs that provide a comprehensive overview of the conflict, from its causes to its aftermath. The museum also has a number of exhibits and displays that highlight the human toll of the revolution, including the impact on civilians, soldiers, and the environment. Despite its sombre subject matter, the Museum of the Revolution is an important and educational institution that provides visitors with a deeper understanding of one of the most significant events in Vietnamese history.

These are some of the best museums in Vietnam that offer a fascinating insight into the country's rich history, culture, and art. Whether you are interested in the country's military heritage, its cultural diversity, or its political and economic development, these museums have something for everyone. So if you are planning a trip to Vietnam, be sure to visit one or more of these institutions, and gain a deeper understanding of the country and its people.

BEST CHURCHES IN VIETNAM

Vietnam is a country with a rich history, culture, and religion, and it is reflected in the number of beautiful and historic churches that can be found throughout the country. In this article, we will highlight some of the best churches in Vietnam that are worth visiting.

1. Notre-Dame Cathedral, Ho Chi Minh City

Notre-Dame Cathedral, also known as Saigon Notre-Dame Cathedral, is one of the most recognizable landmarks in Ho Chi Minh City. The cathedral was built between 1877 and 1880 by French colonists and was initially used as a place of worship for the French community. Today, it serves as a place of worship for both the Catholic and local communities. The cathedral is located in the heart of Ho Chi Minh City and is surrounded by bustling streets and markets.

The cathedral is notable for its Gothic architecture and two 40-metre tall towers, which are visible from many parts of the city. The interior of the cathedral is equally impressive, with stained glass windows, beautiful murals, and intricate wooden carvings. Visitors can also take a look at the antique wooden organ, which is one of the oldest in Southeast Asia.

2. Holy Rosary Cathedral, Hanoi

The Holy Rosary Cathedral, also known as the Hanoi Cathedral, is one of the most beautiful churches in Vietnam and is located in the heart of Hanoi's Old Quarter. The cathedral was built between 1886 and 1901 and was originally used as a place of worship for the French community. Today, it serves as a place of worship for the local Catholic community.

The cathedral is notable for its Gothic-style architecture, which includes a large central tower and two smaller towers, as well as beautiful stained glass windows and intricate carvings. The interior of the cathedral is equally impressive, with soaring ceilings, beautiful stained glass windows, and intricate wooden carvings.

3. St. Joseph's Cathedral, Hanoi

St. Joseph's Cathedral is another beautiful church located in Hanoi, and it is one of the oldest churches in Vietnam. The cathedral was built in the late 19th century and has been used as a place of worship for the Catholic community ever since. The cathedral is notable for its Gothic-style architecture, which includes two large towers and beautiful stained glass windows. The interior of the cathedral is equally impressive, with soaring ceilings, beautiful murals, and intricate wooden carvings.

4. Da Lat Cathedral, Da Lat

Da Lat Cathedral, also known as the Holy Spirit Cathedral, is one of the most beautiful churches in Vietnam and is located in the town of Da Lat. The cathedral was built in the early 20th century and has been used as a place of worship for the local Catholic community ever since. The cathedral is notable for its Gothic-style architecture, which includes two large towers and beautiful stained glass windows. The interior of the cathedral is equally impressive, with soaring ceilings, beautiful murals, and intricate wooden carvings.

5. St. Paul's Church, Hoi An

St. Paul's Church is one of the most historic churches in Vietnam and is located in the town of Hoi An. The church was built in the late 19th century and has been used as a place of worship for the local Catholic community ever since. The church is notable for its Gothic-style architecture, which includes two large towers and beautiful stained glass windows. The interior of the church is equally impressive, with soaring ceilings, beautiful murals, and intricate wooden carvings.

These are just a few of the many beautiful and historic churches in Vietnam that are worth visiting. Each church has its own unique history, architecture

BEST PARKS AND GARDENS IN VIETNAM

Vietnam is a country that is famous for its lush greenery, beautiful beaches, and rolling hills. The country's parks and gardens are a testament to its natural beauty and offer a tranquil escape from the bustling cities. Here are some of the best parks and gardens in Vietnam that you should consider visiting:

1. Tao Dan Park, Ho Chi Minh City: This park is one of the most popular parks in Ho Chi Minh City and is a great place to relax and unwind. It is especially popular among locals who

come here to exercise, play chess, or just enjoy the scenery. The park is also a popular spot for bird-watching and is home to a variety of bird species.

2. Ba Dinh Square, Hanoi: This square is located in the heart of Hanoi and is the site of many important political events and ceremonies. The square is surrounded by lush trees and gardens and is a popular spot for picnics, jogging, and exercise. In the centre of the square is a large statue of Ho Chi Minh, the founder of the communist state of Vietnam.

3. Hoan Kiem Lake, Hanoi: This lake is one of the most famous landmarks in Hanoi and is considered to be a symbol of the city. The lake is surrounded by lush trees and gardens and is a popular spot for walking, jogging, and exercise. There are also several temples and pagodas located around the lake, making it a great

place to explore the cultural and religious heritage of Hanoi.

4. Central Park, Da Nang: This park is located in the heart of Da Nang and is a popular spot for picnics, jogging, and exercise. The park is surrounded by lush trees and gardens and features several lakes and fountains. There are also several recreational facilities,including tennis courts, a swimming pool, and a children's playground, making it a great place to bring the whole family.

5. Bach Thao Park, Hanoi: This park is located in the heart of Hanoi and is one of the city's most popular parks. The park is surrounded by lush trees and gardens and is a popular spot for picnics, jogging, and exercise. The park also features several lakes and fountains and is home to a variety of bird species.

6. Tuoi Tre Park, Ho Chi Minh City: This park is located in the heart of Ho Chi

Minh City and is a popular spot for picnics, jogging, and exercise. The park is surrounded by lush trees and gardens and features several lakes and fountains. The park is also home to a variety of bird species and is a great place to relax and unwind.

7. Dong Ba Market, Hue: This market is located in the heart of Hue and is one of the city's most popular attractions. The market is surrounded by lush trees and gardens and is a popular spot for picnics, jogging, and exercise. The market also features several food stalls and souvenir shops, making it a great place to sample local cuisine and purchase souvenirs.

8. Van Thanh Park, Ho Chi Minh City: This park is located in the heart of Ho Chi Minh City and is a popular spot for picnics, jogging, and exercise. The park is surrounded by lush trees and gardens and features several lakes and fountains. The park is also home to a

variety of bird species and is a great place to relax and unwind.

9. Botanical Garden, Da Lat: This garden is located in Da Lat and is one of the city's most popular attractions. The garden is home to a variety of plants and flowers, including orchids, roses, and lilies. The garden is also home to several walking trails, making it a great place to explore the natural beauty of Da Lat.

10. Hoang Van Thu Park, Phu Quoc: This park is located on the island of Phu Quoc and is a popular spot for picnics, jogging, and exercise. The park is surrounded by lush trees and gardens and features several lakes and fountains. The park is also home to a variety of bird species and is a great place to relax and unwind.

Vietnam is a country that is rich in natural beauty and its parks and gardens offer a peaceful escape from the bustling cities. Whether you're looking to relax, exercise, or explore the local culture, these parks and gardens are a must-visit for anyone visiting Vietnam.

ART GALLERIES IN VIETNAM

Art galleries in Vietnam have undergone a transformation in recent years, reflecting the country's growing interest in contemporary art and its increasing role in the international art world. In the past, traditional Vietnamese art was the focus of galleries and exhibitions, but today, contemporary art is gaining popularity and receiving increased recognition both domestically and abroad.

One of the most notable art galleries in Vietnam is the Vietnam National Museum of Fine Arts in Hanoi. Founded in 1966, the museum is one of the largest art museums in Southeast Asia, showcasing a wide range of traditional and contemporary Vietnamese art. The museum's permanent collection includes works from the 11th century to the present day, including pieces from famous artists such as Nguyen Gia Tri and Le Pho. In addition to its extensive collection, the museum also hosts regular exhibitions and cultural events, making it a popular destination for both art lovers and tourists.

Another important art gallery in Vietnam is the San Art Gallery in Ho Chi Minh City. Founded in 2007, San Art is a non-profit contemporary art organisation that supports emerging and established artists in Vietnam and the surrounding region. The gallery has a reputation for showcasing cutting-edge and experimental works, and has played a key role in promoting contemporary art in Vietnam. San Art also offers residencies, workshops, and other educational programs, helping to nurture and develop the next generation of artists in the country.

The Manzi Art Space in Hanoi is also a major player in the Vietnamese art scene. Founded in 2009, Manzi Art Space is a multi-disciplinary art centre that offers exhibitions, workshops, and other cultural programs. The gallery has a strong focus on contemporary art, and has hosted numerous exhibitions by local and international artists. Manzi Art Space is also a key venue for community events and cultural exchanges, providing a platform for artists and cultural practitioners to connect and collaborate.

In addition to these established art galleries, there are a number of smaller, independent galleries and exhibitions spaces that are making a significant impact on the Vietnamese art scene. For example, The Factory Contemporary Arts Centre in Ho Chi Minh City is a non-profit organization that supports emerging artists and provides a platform for contemporary art exhibitions and cultural programs. The Space SSG in

Hanoi is another noteworthy space that showcases cutting-edge contemporary art and design.

One of the reasons for the growth of the art scene in Vietnam is the country's booming economy. With increasing wealth and greater exposure to international cultural trends, the Vietnamese people have developed a growing interest in contemporary art and design. As a result, the number of galleries, exhibitions, and cultural events has increased, providing a platform for artists to showcase their work and reach new audiences.

Another factor contributing to the growth of the art scene in Vietnam is the increasing recognition of Vietnamese artists on the international stage. In recent years, Vietnamese artists have been featured in major exhibitions around the world, including at the Venice Biennale, the Singapore Art Fair, and Art Basel in Hong Kong. This increased visibility has helped to raise the profile of Vietnamese art and put the country on the map as a major player in the international art world.

The future of the art scene in Vietnam looks bright, with increasing investment from both the government and private sector. For example, the government has recently announced plans to build a major art museum in Ho Chi Minh City, which will be dedicated to showcasing Vietnamese and international contemporary art. This new museum is expected to play a key role in promoting contemporary art in Vietnam and further raising the profile of the country's artists on the international stage.

In conclusion, the art scene in Vietnam has undergone a transformation in recent years, reflecting the country's growing interest in contemporary art and its increasing role in the international art

MUST-DO IN VIETNAM

Vietnam is a stunningly beautiful country with a rich history and culture, making it a must-visit destination for travellers from all over the world. With its unique blend of traditional and modern elements, there is no shortage of things to see, do and experience in this vibrant nation. Here are some of the must-dos in Vietnam that you should consider when planning your trip.

1. Explore Hanoi: The capital city of Hanoi is a fascinating blend of old and new, with its narrow streets, ancient temples and colonial-style architecture. Start your visit by exploring the bustling Old Quarter, where you'll find shops and street vendors selling everything from traditional clothing to spices. Don't

miss Hoan Kiem Lake, a tranquil urban oasis in the heart of the city, and the iconic Temple of Literature, which is dedicated to Confucius.

2. Visit Halong Bay: This stunning bay is a UNESCO World Heritage site and one of the most popular attractions in Vietnam. With its towering limestone cliffs and crystal-clear waters, Halong Bay is a true natural wonder. Take a boat tour to explore the bay and its many islands, and make sure to stop at the Sung Sot Cave, which is one of the largest and most spectacular caves in the region.

3. Discover Hoi An: This charming town is a must-visit destination for those who want to experience a traditional Vietnamese lifestyle. With its well-preserved architecture and narrow streets, Hoi An is a true cultural gem. Take a stroll through the Old Town and visit some of the local artisan workshops, where you can see

traditional crafts being made. You can also enjoy a scenic bike ride along the Thu Bon River or visit the ancient Japanese Bridge, one of the most famous landmarks in Hoi An.

4. Sample the Cuisine: Vietnamese cuisine is a delicious and unique blend of flavours and ingredients. Try some of the country's most famous dishes, such as pho (a noodle soup), banh mi (a sandwich made with a baguette), and bún chả (grilled pork with noodles). Make sure to also try some of the local street food, which is an experience in itself.

5. Experience the History: Vietnam has a rich and fascinating history that has been shaped by centuries of war and conflict. Visit the War Remnants Museum in Ho Chi Minh City, which showcases the country's recent history and the impact of the Vietnam War. You can also visit the Cu Chi Tunnels, which were used by the Viet Cong

during the war, or take a tour of the ancient citadel of Hue, which was the former imperial capital of Vietnam.

6. Explore the Mekong Delta: The Mekong Delta is one of the most important agricultural regions in Vietnam, and it is a must-visit destination for those interested in the country's rural life. Take a boat tour through the network of waterways that make up the delta, and visit local villages, where you can see how the local people live and work. You can also taste some of the fresh local produce, such as fruit, vegetables, and seafood.

7. Visit Sapa: Sapa is a picturesque mountain town located in the northern part of Vietnam, and it is a popular destination for trekkers and adventure seekers. With its rolling hills and stunning views of the surrounding mountains, Sapa is a true natural wonder. Take a trek through

the nearby rice terraces, visit the local ethnic minority villages, or simply relax and enjoy the stunning scenery.

8. Experience the Culture: Vietnam is a country with a rich cultural heritage, and there are many ways to experience it. Visit a traditional Vietnamese water puppet show, which is a unique art form that has been passed down for generations. Take a cooking class to learn how to make traditional Vietnamese dishes, or visit one of the country's many festivals and markets, where you can see local people celebrating and selling their wares. You can also visit a temple or pagoda to learn about the country's religious beliefs and practices, or attend a traditional music or dance performance.

9. Visit the Central Highlands: The Central Highlands of Vietnam are a stunning region of rolling hills and lush forests, and they are a popular

destination for adventure and outdoor enthusiasts. Take a scenic drive through the hills, explore the local markets, or visit one of the area's many waterfalls and hot springs. You can also go trekking or mountain biking through the rugged terrain, or visit a local coffee or tea plantation to learn about the area's thriving agriculture.

10. Take a Motorbike Tour: A motorbike tour is one of the best ways to explore the country and experience its unique landscapes and culture. With its winding roads, beautiful scenery, and friendly locals, Vietnam is a motor biker's paradise. Rent a motorbike and set off on your own, or join a guided tour for a more structured and safe experience.

These are just a few of the many must-dos in Vietnam, and there is truly something for everyone in this fascinating and diverse country. Whether you're interested in history, culture, nature, or adventure, Vietnam has it all and more. So plan your trip today, and discover the many wonders that await you in this beautiful and vibrant nation.

CHAPTER TWO

TRAVEL SMART

THINGS TO KNOW BEFORE VISITING VIETNAM

If you are planning a trip to Vietnam, here are some things you should know before visiting:

1. Climate: Vietnam has a tropical climate, with hot and humid weather throughout the year. The best time to visit is during the dry season, which lasts from October to April, when temperatures are more moderate. The monsoon season, which runs from May to September, can bring heavy rain and floods to some parts of the country.

2. Culture: Vietnam is a country with a long and rich cultural heritage, with

influences from China, France, and other countries. It is important to be respectful of local customs and traditions, including traditional dress codes, such as covering up your legs and arms, and removing your shoes when entering a temple or someone's home.

3. Food: Vietnamese cuisine is a delicious blend of fresh ingredients and flavorful spices. Popular dishes include pho (noodle soup), banh mi (sandwich), and spring rolls. Street food is also a big part of Vietnamese culture and can be a great way to experience the local food culture.

4. Currency: The currency used in Vietnam is the Vietnamese Dong (VND). It is best to exchange your money into Dong before arriving in the country, as ATMs may not be widely available in some areas.

5. Transportation: Vietnam has an extensive network of buses, trains, and

flights that connect the different cities and regions of the country. Taxis are also available in major cities, but it's best to use reputable companies and agree on a fare before starting the journey.

6. Health and safety: Vietnam is generally a safe country to visit, but as with any foreign country, it is important to take precautions to ensure your health and safety. Make sure you are up to date on your vaccinations, bring appropriate medications, and stay hydrated in the hot and humid weather.

7. Language: The official language of Vietnam is Vietnamese, but many people in tourist areas also speak English. It is helpful to learn a few key phrases in Vietnamese to communicate with the local people and make your trip more enjoyable.

8. Shopping: Vietnam is famous for its markets, where you can buy

everything from local souvenirs to handmade crafts. Haggling is common, so be prepared to negotiate prices.

9. Adventure and outdoor activities: Vietnam offers a range of outdoor activities, including trekking, kayaking, rock climbing, and scuba diving. The country is also home to stunning natural scenery, including mountains, beaches, and national parks, making it an ideal destination for adventure and outdoor enthusiasts.

10. History and war sites: Vietnam has a long and complex history, including a history of conflict and war. Visitors can visit the War Remnants Museum in Ho Chi Minh City, the Cu Chi Tunnels near Saigon, and the Hoa Lo Prison in Hanoi, which provide an insight into the country's recent history and the impact of the Vietnam War.

11. Accommodation: Vietnam offers a range of accommodation options, from budget-friendly hostels to luxurious five-star hotels. In tourist areas, there is a good selection of hotels, but it is best to book in advance during peak season.

12. Visa requirements: Most foreign visitors to Vietnam need a visa to enter the country, which can be obtained through a Vietnamese embassy or consulate or through a visa-on-arrival service. The type of visa required and the length of stay will depend on the purpose of your trip.

13. Tipping: Tipping is not expected in Vietnam, but it is becoming more common in tourist areas. If you receive good service, it is considered polite to leave a small amount of money as a tip, usually around 10% of the total bill.

14. Respect for elders: Vietnam is a country with strong family values, and it is considered respectful to show deference to elders. This includes not talking over or interrupting them, and offering them the best seat or food.
15. Smoking and drinking: Smoking is prevalent in Vietnam, and it is common to see people smoking in public places. Drinking alcohol is also part of the local culture, but it is important to be mindful of local laws and customs, especially in terms of public behaviour and drinking in moderation.
16. Local customs: Vietnam is a conservative country, and it is important to dress modestly and avoid public displays of affection. When visiting religious sites, it is also important to remove your shoes and be respectful of local customs.
17. Festivals and events: Vietnam is a country that celebrates many festivals

and events throughout the year, including Tet (Vietnamese New Year), the Mid-Autumn Festival, and the Hoi An Lantern Festival. These events are a great opportunity to experience local culture and tradition, and it is recommended to plan your trip around one of these events to make the most of your experience.

18.   Photography: Vietnam is a visually stunning country, and many visitors enjoy taking photographs of their experiences. However, it is important to be mindful of local customs and laws, especially when taking photographs of people, military sites, and government buildings.

By keeping these things in mind, you can ensure a smooth and enjoyable trip, and make the most of your time in this fascinating country.

TRAVEL OPTIONS

Vietnam is a beautiful country with a rich culture and history, making it a popular tourist destination. The country offers a diverse range of landscapes and experiences, from the bustling cities to the tranquil countryside, making it a must-visit for travellers. With so many options for travel, it can be overwhelming to decide how to get around and what to see. I will discuss the various travel options to Vietnam and the best way to explore the country.

1. Flying to Vietnam

Flying is the most convenient way to reach Vietnam, with several international airports in the country, including Hanoi (Noi Bai International Airport) and Ho Chi Minh City (Tan Son Nhat International Airport). Both cities are well connected to major cities around the world, and there are many airlines operating flights to Vietnam. You can find direct flights from many countries, including the United States, Australia, and Europe. If you are travelling from within Asia, there are also many regional airlines that offer flights to Vietnam.

2. Overland Travel

For those who prefer overland travel, it is possible to enter Vietnam from neighbouring countries such as Cambodia, Laos, and China. This is a good option for those who want to see more of the region and experience different cultures. From Cambodia, you can cross the border at Bavet/Moc Bai and continue on to Ho Chi Minh City. From Laos, you can cross the border at Nam Can/Cau Treo and continue on to Hanoi. From China, you can cross the border at Lao Cai/Hekou and continue on to Hanoi. Overland travel can be a more budget-friendly option, and it also offers a different perspective on the country and its culture.

3. Train Travel

Train travel is a popular option for those who want to see more of the country and take in the scenery at a slower pace. Vietnam has a well-developed railway system, and trains run regularly between major cities such as Hanoi and Ho Chi Minh City. There are also several scenic train routes that offer breathtaking views of the countryside. Some of the most popular trains include the Reunification Express and the North-South Express. Train travel in Vietnam can be a great way to experience the local culture, meet new people, and see the countryside.

4. Bus Travel

Bus travel is a popular and budget-friendly option for those who want to see more of the country. Buses run regularly between major cities and towns, and there are many options for long-distance and local buses. Buses in Vietnam are comfortable and air-conditioned, and they offer a convenient way to see the country without breaking the bank. However, bus travel can be a bit more time-consuming than other forms of transportation, and the roads can be congested during peak hours.

5. Private Car and Driver

For those who want more flexibility and control over their itinerary, a private car and driver is a good option. This allows you to travel at your own pace and explore the country at your leisure. You can choose to rent a car, or you can hire a driver to take you around. A private car and driver can be more expensive than other forms of transportation, but it offers a level of comfort and convenience that is hard to match.

6. Motorbike and Bicycle Rentals

For those who want to experience the country on a more personal level, motorbike and bicycle rentals are a good option. This allows you to explore the countryside and small villages at your own pace, and to get off the beaten path. Motorbike and bicycle rentals are widely available in Vietnam, and they offer a fun and adventurous way to see the country. However, it is important to note that the roads in Vietnam can be challenging, with heavy traffic and limited infrastructure in some areas. It is recommended to have some experience riding a motorbike or bicycle before attempting this type of travel.

When choosing a travel option in Vietnam, it is important to consider your budget, the amount of time you have, and your personal preferences. For example, flying is a quick and convenient option, but it can be more expensive. On the other hand, overland travel and train travel are more budget-friendly options, but they can take longer and may not be as comfortable.

Another important factor to consider is the time of year you plan to visit Vietnam. The country has a tropical climate, with a hot and humid summer and a cool and dry winter. The best time to visit Vietnam depends on the type of weather and experiences you are looking for. For example, the summer months are ideal for beach-goers, while the winter months are best for exploring the cities and the countryside.

In conclusion, Vietnam is a wonderful country with a wealth of travel options. Whether you choose to fly, travel overland, take the train, or explore on a motorbike, you are sure to have an amazing experience. The country has something to offer for every traveller, from bustling cities to tranquil countryside, and from rich history to stunning landscapes. So why not start planning your next adventure to Vietnam today?

GETTING HERE AND AROUND

Transportation in Vietnam has come a long way since the days of bicycles and horse-drawn carts. The country's modern transportation infrastructure has significantly improved, especially since the 1990s, with increased investment in highways, airports, and seaports. Today, Vietnam boasts of a well-developed transportation system that is convenient, affordable, and efficient.

Road Transportation

Road transportation is the most widely used mode of transportation in Vietnam, with millions of people relying on it every day to get to work, school, or run errands. The country's road network comprises over 100,000 km of highways, including both national and provincial roads. The majority of roads in Vietnam are two-lane highways, although some sections have been expanded to four lanes.

One of the most significant investments in road transportation in Vietnam was the construction of the North-South Expressway. This highway, which spans over 1,700 km, connects Hanoi in the north to Ho Chi Minh City in the south, providing a smooth and convenient road connection between the two major cities. The highway has been instrumental in reducing travel time between the two cities, allowing people to move faster and more efficiently.

Another important road infrastructure project in Vietnam is the National Highway 1A. This highway is the longest in the country and runs from Hanoi in the north to Ho Chi Minh City in the south, passing through several provinces along the way. The highway is considered the backbone of the country's road transportation network and is an essential route for commercial goods and passenger transportation.

Motorbikes are the most common form of transportation in Vietnam, and the roads are filled with them. Motorbikes are an affordable and convenient mode of transportation, allowing people to get around quickly and easily. However, the high number of motorbikes on the roads also results in traffic congestion and a high number of road accidents.

Buses are another popular mode of transportation in Vietnam. The country has a vast network of inter-city and intra-city buses that connect major cities and towns. Buses are an affordable and convenient way to travel long distances, with most cities having several bus stations that serve both local and long-distance routes. However, the quality of the bus services can vary greatly, with some being well-maintained and air-conditioned, while others can be cramped and in poor condition.

Rail Transportation

Rail transportation in Vietnam is less developed compared to road transportation, with a limited rail network that spans over 1,600 km. The country's rail network mainly serves the northern and central regions, connecting major cities like Hanoi, Haiphong, and Danang. The rail system in Vietnam is undergoing expansion and modernization, with plans to extend the network and improve the quality of services.

The most important railway route in Vietnam is the North-South Railway, which connects Hanoi in the north to Ho Chi Minh City in the south. The railway provides an alternative to road transportation, especially for long-distance travel, and is considered a faster and more comfortable mode of transportation. However, the quality of rail services can vary, with some trains being modern and well-maintained, while others can be in poor condition.

Air Transportation

Air transportation has become increasingly important in Vietnam, especially in recent years, with the country's aviation sector experiencing significant growth. The country's aviation network comprises over

25 airports, including both international and domestic airports. The largest and busiest airport in Vietnam is Tan Son Nhat International Airport in Ho Chi Minh City, which handles the majority of the country's international flights.

Vietnam's aviation sector has seen significant investment in recent years, with several new airlines entering the market and the development of new airports and the expansion of existing ones. This has resulted in increased competition and lower airfares, making air travel more affordable and accessible to more people.

Domestic air travel has become an important mode of transportation in Vietnam, with several airlines operating flights between major cities and tourist destinations. Domestic air travel is particularly useful for travellers who want to save time on their journeys, especially in the case of long-distance travel.

International air travel is also growing in Vietnam, with several airlines operating flights to and from the country. The development of new airports, such as the new Long Thanh International Airport near Ho Chi Minh City, is expected to increase the country's international connectivity and attract more international airlines to operate in Vietnam.

Water Transportation

Water transportation is an important mode of transportation in Vietnam, particularly in the delta and coastal regions, where rivers and waterways are a vital means of transportation. The country has a well-developed network of waterways, including both rivers and canals, that serve as important routes for goods transportation and passenger services.

Ferries and boats are common modes of water transportation in Vietnam, especially in the delta and coastal regions. They are an affordable and convenient way to travel, with many boats operating regular services between towns and villages. The country also has several large river ports, such as the Saigon Port in Ho Chi Minh City and the Hanoi Port in Hanoi, that serve as major hubs for goods transportation.

Urban Transportation

Urban transportation in Vietnam is a major challenge, particularly in large cities like Hanoi and Ho Chi Minh City, where traffic congestion is a significant problem. The increasing population and economic growth in these cities have led to an increase in the number of vehicles on the roads, resulting in traffic jams and long travel times.

To tackle the issue of traffic congestion, several cities in Vietnam have implemented measures to encourage the use of public transportation. This includes the development of new metro systems, such as the Hanoi Metro and the Ho Chi Minh City Metro, as well as the expansion of bus services and the introduction of new bus rapid transit systems.

ESSENTIALS

Vietnam is a beautiful country with a rich cultural heritage, stunning landscapes, and delicious cuisine. Whether you are planning a trip to Vietnam for the first time or you have been there before, there are certain essentials you should carry with you to ensure a smooth and enjoyable trip. In this article, we will discuss the top things you should consider carrying with you when visiting Vietnam.

1. Passport and visas: This is the most important document you need to carry with you when visiting Vietnam. Your passport should be valid for at least six months from the date of entry, and you may need to obtain a visa prior to your trip. You can obtain a visa through a Vietnamese embassy or consulate, or through an online visa service.

2. Cash: While credit and debit cards are widely accepted in Vietnam, it's always a good idea to carry some cash with you. The local currency in Vietnam is the Vietnamese Dong (VND), and it is

recommended to have a mix of smaller and larger denominations. You can exchange currency at banks, hotels, and money exchange kiosks.

3. Travel insurance: Travel insurance is essential when travelling to Vietnam, especially if you are planning to participate in any adventure activities such as trekking, kayaking, or scuba diving. Travel insurance will protect you in case of any accidents, illness, or theft.

4. Mobile phone and charger: It's important to carry a mobile phone with you when travelling in Vietnam, as it can be very useful for navigation, making reservations, or communicating with others. You can also buy a local SIM card upon arrival, which will give you access to data and calling services.

5. Camera: Vietnam is a visually stunning country, and you will want to capture the memories of your trip. A

camera, whether it is a traditional film camera or a digital camera, is a must-have item for capturing the beautiful landscapes and cultural experiences.

6. First aid kit: A basic first aid kit can be very useful in case of any minor injuries or illnesses. You should carry pain relief medication, antiseptics, bandages, and any other medications you may need.

7. Clothing: When packing for your trip to Vietnam, it is important to consider the weather and cultural norms. Vietnam has a tropical climate, so lightweight and breathable clothing is recommended. It is also important to be respectful of local customs, so avoiding revealing clothing is advisable.

8. Water bottle: Staying hydrated is crucial when travelling, especially in a hot and humid climate like Vietnam. Carrying a reusable water bottle with

you is a great way to reduce plastic waste and save money on bottled water.

9. Umbrella or rain jacket: Vietnam is known for its rainy season, which usually occurs from May to September. Carrying an umbrella or a lightweight rain jacket can help protect you from the rain and keep you dry.

10. Sunscreen: Vietnam is close to the equator, so the sun can be very strong. Sunscreen with a high SPF is essential to protect your skin from sunburn and skin damage.

11. Mosquito repellent: Mosquitoes can be a problem in Vietnam, especially during the rainy season. Carrying a mosquito repellent is important to prevent insect bites and reduce the risk of diseases such as dengue fever or malaria.

12. Portable charger: Having a portable charger with you can be very useful in

case your mobile phone or camera runs out of battery while you are on the go.

13. Personal hygiene products: It's always a good idea to carry personal hygiene products such as wet wipes, hand sanitizer, and tissues with you when travelling.

WHAT TO WEAR FOR EVERY SEASON IN VIETNAM

Vietnam is a country located in Southeast Asia, and it has a tropical climate with high humidity and temperatures throughout the year. The country experiences three main seasons: the hot and dry season from March to May, the rainy season from June to September, and the cool and dry season from October to February. To help you prepare for your trip to Vietnam, this guide will provide information on what to wear for each of these seasons, taking into account both the weather conditions and cultural norms.

Spring (March to May)

Spring in Vietnam is hot and dry, with temperatures ranging from 27°C to 35°C (80°F to 95°F). During this time, it is common for the sun to be shining and the skies to be clear. To stay cool in the warm weather, lightweight, breathable clothing is recommended. Cotton, linen, and rayon are all good choices, as they will keep you comfortable and cool throughout the day.

For women, sundresses, shorts, and T-shirts are popular options. It's a good idea to wear light-coloured clothing, as darker colours will attract more heat. Avoid wearing tight or heavy clothing, as these will make you feel hot and uncomfortable. Sandals or open-toed shoes are also recommended, as they will allow your feet to breathe and stay cool.

For men, lightweight pants or shorts, along with a T-shirt or a short-sleeved shirt, will keep you comfortable in the spring weather. Light-coloured clothing is also recommended for men, and it's best to avoid wearing heavy clothing, such as jeans or sweatshirts, as these will make you feel hot and uncomfortable. Shoes such as sandals or loafers are also a good choice, as they will keep your feet cool and comfortable.

Summer (June to September)

Summer in Vietnam is the rainy season, and temperatures range from 27°C to 35°C (80°F to 95°F). During this time, it's common for there to be heavy rains and high humidity, so it's important to wear clothing that will keep you cool and dry. Lightweight, breathable fabrics are recommended, such as cotton, linen, and rayon.

For women, lightweight dresses, skirts, and shorts are popular options. It's best to avoid wearing tight clothing, as this will make you feel hot and uncomfortable in the high humidity. A raincoat or umbrella is also a must, as it will protect you from the rain. Sandals or closed-toe shoes are recommended, as they will keep your feet dry in case of rain.

For men, lightweight pants or shorts, along with a T-shirt or a short-sleeved shirt, are popular options. Again, it's best to avoid tight clothing, as this will make you feel hot and uncomfortable in the high humidity. A raincoat or umbrella is also necessary, and closed-toe shoes are recommended to keep your feet dry in case of rain.

Fall (October to February)

Fall in Vietnam is cool and dry, with temperatures ranging from 20°C to 25°C (68°F to 77°F). During this time, it's common for the skies to be clear and the weather to be pleasant, making it a great time to visit the country. Lightweight clothing is still recommended, but you can add a few layering pieces to your outfit, such as a lightweight sweater or a denim jacket, to stay warm in the cool weather.

For women, dresses, skirts, and pants are all good options. Light-coloured clothing is recommended, as darker colours will absorb more heat. Light jackets, such as denim jackets or cardigans,can be added to your outfit to stay warm when the temperatures drop. Boots or closed-toe shoes are a good choice, as they will keep your feet warm and protected from the cooler weather.

For men, pants or khaki shorts, along with a long-sleeved shirt or a lightweight sweater, are popular options. A light jacket or sweater is recommended, as it will keep you warm in the cool weather. Closed-toe shoes, such as sneakers or loafers, are also a good choice, as they will keep your feet warm and protected from the cool weather.

Cultural Considerations

In addition to taking into account the weather conditions, it's also important to consider cultural norms when dressing in Vietnam. Vietnamese people tend to dress modestly and conservatively, especially when visiting religious sites or rural areas. Women should avoid wearing revealing clothing, such as short shorts or low-cut tops, and men should avoid wearing sleeveless shirts. When visiting religious sites, such as temples or pagodas, it's also important to dress respectfully, covering your arms and legs and removing your shoes before entering.

When travelling to Vietnam, it's important to take into account the weather conditions and cultural norms when deciding what to wear. Lightweight, breathable clothing is recommended in all seasons, with the addition of layering pieces in the cooler months. It's also important to consider cultural norms, dressing modestly and conservatively, especially when visiting religious sites or rural areas. By following these guidelines, you can ensure that you stay comfortable and respectful during your travels in Vietnam.

HELPFUL VIETNAMESE PHRASES
As a tourist, it's always a good idea to learn some basic Vietnamese phrases that can come in handy while travelling in the country. We'll be discussing some essential

Vietnamese phrases that can help you communicate better with the locals and make your travel experience more enjoyable.

Hello/Goodbye:

1. The most basic and essential phrase that you must know while travelling in Vietnam is "Xin chào" (sin-chow), which means hello. Another way of greeting people is "Chào" (chow) which is used informally. To say goodbye, you can use "Tạm biệt" (tam-bee-et) which means farewell.

Yes/No:

2. "Có" (co) means yes and "Không" (khong) means no. These two phrases are the most commonly used words in

Vietnam and can come in handy in various situations.
Thank you/You're welcome:

3. "Cảm ơn" (kam-uhn) is used to express gratitude and means thank you. To respond to a thank you, you can use "Không có gì" (khong co gee), which means you're welcome.

Excuse me:

4. "Xin lỗi" (sin-loy) is used to apologise or to get someone's attention. It's a polite way to start a conversation with someone in Vietnam.

How much?

5. "Bao nhiêu?" (bao-nee-yuu) is used to ask about the price of something and is an essential phrase for bargaining in local markets.

How are you?

6. "Bạn cảm thấy như thế nào?" (ban kam tay nuu tay now) is used to ask someone how they are feeling. It's a polite and friendly way to start a conversation with someone in Vietnam.

I don't understand:

7. "Tôi không hiểu" (toy khong hieu) is used to express that you don't understand something that someone has said to you.

Can you speak English?

8. "Bạn có nói tiếng Anh không?" (ban co noi tieng ahn khong) is used to ask someone if they speak English. Knowing this phrase can help you find someone who can assist you in case you need help communicating in Vietnam.

Where is the restroom?

9. "Nhà vệ sinh ở đâu?" (na veh sinh oh dau) is used to ask for the location of the restroom.

Can I have a glass of water?

10. "Tôi có thể có một cốc nước không?" (toy co theh co mot coch nook khong) is used to ask for a glass of water.

Do you have this in a different size/colour?

11. "Bạn có cái này có kích thước/màu khác không?" (ban co cai nay co keech twok/mau khak khong?) is used to ask if a store has an item in a different size or color.

How do I get to...?

12. "Tôi phải đi đến... thì phải làm sao?" (toy fai dee den... tee fai lahm sao?) is used to ask for directions to a particular place.

Can you help me?

13. "Bạn có thể giúp tôi không?" (ban co theh joop toy khong?) is a phrase used to ask for help from someone.

Can I have the bill, please?

14. "Tôi có thể nhận hoá đơn, xin vui lòng?" (toy co theh nhan hoa don, sin vway lohng?) is used to request the bill at a restaurant.

How do you say ... in Vietnamese?

15. "Tại sao bạn nói... trong tiếng Việt?" (tie sao ban noi... trong ting vyet?) is used to ask how to say a particular word in Vietnamese.

Do you have any recommendations?

16. "Bạn có gợi ý gì không?" (ban co goy yee gee khong?) is used to ask for recommendations, whether it be for food, activities, or places to visit.

These are some of the most helpful Vietnamese phrases for tourists. While travelling in Vietnam, it's always a good idea to carry a phrasebook or download a language translation app to help you communicate better with the locals. Remember, even a small effort to speak the local language can go a long way in making a positive impression and making your travel experience more enjoyable.

SAFETY AND SECURITY

Vietnam is a Southeast Asian country located in the Indochinese Peninsula and is bordered by China to the north, Laos to the northwest, and Cambodia to the southwest. With a population of over 97 million people, it is one of the most populous countries in the region. In recent years, the country has experienced tremendous economic growth, with the tourism industry playing a significant role in driving the country's development. I will discuss the safety and security situation in Vietnam as of 2021.

Safety in Vietnam:

Vietnam is considered a relatively safe country for tourists, and crime rates are low compared to other countries in the region. However, it is important for visitors to take necessary precautions, such as avoiding dark and deserted areas and not carrying large amounts of cash. Petty crimes, such as pickpocketing and theft, can occur in tourist areas, so it is recommended to keep a close eye on personal belongings, especially in crowded places such as markets and tourist sites.

Visitors should also exercise caution when using ATMs and be aware of skimming devices that can steal credit card information. It is also advisable to use ATMs located inside banks or shopping centres, as these are typically more secure than standalone ATMs.

Traffic in Vietnam can be chaotic, and accidents are common. Visitors should be aware of the local driving culture and exercise caution when crossing roads or cycling. It is also recommended to wear a helmet when riding a motorbike or bicycle.

Security in Vietnam:

Vietnam is generally considered a politically stable country, and the government has a good track record of maintaining peace and order. However, visitors should be aware of the country's history and be mindful of the sensitive political and social issues that may arise during their visit.

The Vietnamese government has taken measures to enhance the country's security, and the police force is highly visible and present in major cities. The government also cooperates with international organisations to prevent terrorism and to ensure the safety of tourists.

Visitors should be aware of the country's visa requirements and be mindful of local laws and customs. Vietnam has strict drug laws, and visitors found possessing or trafficking drugs can face severe penalties, including imprisonment.

Visitors should also be aware of the country's internet censorship laws and avoid accessing restricted websites or engaging in any political or controversial activities that may be perceived as a threat to the country's security.

Vietnam is generally considered a safe and secure country for tourists. Visitors should exercise caution, be mindful of local laws and customs, and take necessary precautions to ensure a safe and enjoyable visit. By being aware of the potential risks and taking steps to minimise them, visitors can have a memorable and safe experience in Vietnam.

GREAT ITINERARIES

Here are a few great itineraries for Vietnam:

Hanoi and Halong Bay (4-5 days)

1. Start your trip in Hanoi, the capital of Vietnam, and spend a few days exploring the city's cultural and historical landmarks, such as the Ho Chi Minh Mausoleum, the Temple of Literature, and the Old Quarter. Then, take a two-day cruise on Halong Bay, a stunning natural wonder with

thousands of limestone islands and crystal-clear water.

Ho Chi Minh City and Mekong Delta (4-5 days)

2. Explore the vibrant city of Ho Chi Minh (formerly Saigon), where you can visit the War Remnants Museum, the Notre Dame Cathedral, and the bustling Ben Thanh Market. Then, take a day trip to the Mekong Delta, a region known for its floating markets, fruit orchards, and traditional handicrafts.

Hoi An and Hue (3-4 days)

3. Hoi An is a charming coastal town known for its well-preserved historic architecture, delicious food, and beautiful beaches. Spend a few days

exploring the town's ancient temples and pagodas, taking a cooking class, and relaxing on the beach. Then, head to Hue, the former imperial capital of Vietnam, and visit the city's citadel, tombs of the emperors, and Thien Mu Pagoda.

Sapa and Bac Ha (4-5 days)

4. Sapa is a mountain town in northern Vietnam known for its stunning rice terraces and ethnic minority villages. Take a trek through the hills, visit local markets, and learn about the unique cultures of the region. Then, head to Bac Ha, a small town known for its Sunday market, where you can see the traditional dress and crafts of the Flower Hmong and other ethnic groups.

Phu Quoc Island (3-4 days)

5. For a more relaxed and beach-focused trip, head to Phu Quoc Island, located in the Gulf of Thailand. The island has beautiful beaches, clear waters, and great snorkelling and diving opportunities. You can also explore local fishing villages, visit a pearl farm, or take a hike in the national park.

These are just a few examples of the many itineraries you can create in Vietnam. With its diverse landscapes, rich culture, and delicious food, there is something for every type of traveller.

CHAPTER THREE

ACCOMODATIONS

BEST PLACES TO EAT ,SLEEP AND RELAX

Vietnam is a country known for its rich culture, history, and diverse cuisine. From bustling cities to serene rural landscapes, Vietnam has a lot to offer to travellers seeking to eat, sleep, and relax in the country. Here are some of the best places to consider when visiting Vietnam.

Eating in Vietnam:

1. Hanoi - Hanoi is considered by many to be the cultural and culinary capital of Vietnam. It is famous for its street food, which can be found in the city's many food markets and street stalls. Must-try dishes include pho (noodle

soup), bun cha (grilled pork and noodles), banh mi (Vietnamese sandwich), and egg coffee.

2. Hue - Hue is a former imperial city in central Vietnam and is known for its royal cuisine. The city has a long history of royal cuisine that is distinct from other regions. Dishes like banh khoai (fried pancake), banh bot loc (shrimp dumplings), and bun bo Hue (spicy beef noodle soup) are popular here.

3. Hoi An - Hoi An is a small, charming town located on the central coast of Vietnam. It is famous for its ancient architecture, lanterns, and delicious food. Local specialties include cao lau (noodles with pork and herbs), mi quang (tumeric noodles with shrimp and pork), and white rose dumplings (shrimp-filled rice cakes).

4. Saigon (Ho Chi Minh City) - Saigon is the largest city in Vietnam and is a melting pot of different cultures and

cuisines. It is home to some of the best restaurants in the country, offering everything from traditional Vietnamese food to international cuisine. Must-try dishes include banh xeo (Vietnamese crepes), com tam (broken rice), and bun bo Hue.

Sleeping in Vietnam:

1. Hanoi - Hanoi offers a wide range of accommodations, from budget hostels to luxury hotels. Staying in the Old Quarter is recommended for its convenient location and historic charm.
2. Sapa - Sapa is a small town in the northwest of Vietnam known for its beautiful rice terraces and mountain scenery. It is a popular destination for hiking and trekking and offers a range of accommodations, from homestays to luxury resorts.

3. Hue - Hue has a range of accommodation options, including traditional homestays, budget hotels, and luxury resorts. Staying in a traditional homestay is recommended to experience local life and cuisine.
4. Hoi An - Hoi An offers a range of accommodations, from budget hostels to luxury resorts. Staying in a hotel or homestay near the ancient town is recommended for its proximity to the town's attractions.

Relaxing in Vietnam:

1. Ha Long Bay - Ha Long Bay is a UNESCO World Heritage Site and is known for its stunning limestone karsts and calm waters. Taking a cruise through the bay is a popular way to relax and take in the scenery.
2. Nha Trang - Nha Trang is a coastal city in central Vietnam known for its

beaches and water sports. Relaxing on the beach or taking a boat tour to nearby islands are popular activities.

3. Mekong Delta - The Mekong Delta is a vast network of rivers and canals in southern Vietnam. Taking a boat tour through the delta and visiting local villages is a great way to relax and experience local life.

4. Phu Quoc Island - Phu Quoc Island is a beautiful island in the Gulf of Thailand known for its pristine beaches and tranquil atmosphere. Relaxing on the beach or taking a boat tour to nearby islands are popular activities.

Vietnam is a beautiful and diverse country with a lot to offer for those seeking to eat,

ENTERTAINMENT AND NIGHTLIFE

Over the years, the country has developed a thriving entertainment and nightlife scene, particularly in its major cities such as Ho

Chi Minh City (formerly known as Saigon), Hanoi, and Da Nang.

Entertainment

Vietnam has a diverse range of entertainment options for locals and tourists alike. From traditional performances to modern activities, there is something for everyone.

1. Traditional Performances

One of the best ways to experience Vietnam's culture is through traditional performances. These performances typically include music, dance, and theatre and showcase the country's unique customs and traditions. Popular traditional performances include water puppetry, a unique form of puppetry that originated in North Vietnam, and cai luong, a type of Vietnamese opera.

2. Theme Parks and Amusement Parks

Vietnam has a number of theme parks and amusement parks that provide fun-filled entertainment for families and thrill-seekers. Some of the most popular ones include Dam Sen Water Park in Ho Chi Minh City, Vinpearl Land in Nha Trang, and Sun World in Da Nang.

3. Cinemas

Cinemas are popular in Vietnam and can be found in most major cities. While Hollywood movies are widely popular, there is also a growing Vietnamese film industry that produces high-quality films. In addition to traditional cinemas, there are also outdoor cinemas that offer a unique experience.

4. Music and Festivals

Music is an important part of Vietnamese culture, and the country has a vibrant music scene. There are several music festivals throughout the year, including the Hanoi Sound Stuff Festival and the Quest Festival. These festivals attract both local and international artists and provide an opportunity to experience different types of music.

Nightlife

Vietnam's nightlife has developed rapidly over the past few decades, and major cities like Ho Chi Minh City and Hanoi have become hotspots for nightlife entertainment. Here are some of the most popular nightlife options in Vietnam:

1. Bars and Nightclubs

Bars and nightclubs are a popular nightlife option in Vietnam, particularly in Ho Chi

Minh City and Hanoi. There are a wide variety of bars and nightclubs, from upscale venues to budget-friendly options. Popular venues include Chill Skybar and Lush in Ho Chi Minh City and Dragonfly in Hanoi.

2. Rooftop Bars

Rooftop bars have become increasingly popular in Vietnam, providing a unique way to experience the city skyline. Popular rooftop bars include Saigon Saigon Bar in Ho Chi Minh City and Top of Hanoi in Hanoi.

3. Karaoke

Karaoke is a popular pastime in Vietnam, and there are numerous karaoke bars throughout the country. These bars offer private rooms where groups of friends can sing and enjoy drinks and snacks.

4. Street Food

Street food is an important part of Vietnam's culture and is a popular nightlife option. Night markets, such as Ben Thanh Market in Ho Chi Minh City, offer a variety of street food options, including banh mi (Vietnamese sandwich), pho (Vietnamese noodle soup), and spring rolls.

Vietnam offers a diverse range of entertainment and nightlife options that cater to a variety of interests and budgets. Whether you want to experience traditional performances, enjoy theme parks, or explore the city's nightlife, Vietnam has something for everyone.

CHAPTER FOUR

FUN FACTS ABOUT VIETNAM

1. Vietnam is the world's 15th most populous country, with over 97 million people.
2. The Vietnamese language has six different tones, which can completely change the meaning of a word.
3. Vietnam is the second-largest coffee producer in the world after Brazil.
4. The Vietnamese name for their country is "Viet Nam," which means "people living in the south."
5. Vietnam has a coastline that is over 3,200 kilometres long, with some of the most beautiful beaches in Southeast Asia.

6. The world's largest cave, Son Doong, is located in Vietnam and is over 5.5 miles long.
7. The national animal of Vietnam is the water buffalo.
8. The traditional Vietnamese dress for women is called "Ao Dai," which is a long tunic with pants underneath.
9. Vietnam is the largest exporter of cashew nuts in the world.
10. The Vietnamese currency is called the dong.
11. Vietnam has a very young population, with over half of the population under the age of 35.
12. The Vietnamese love to play a game called "O An Quan," which is a traditional board game that is similar to Mancala.
13. The Vietnamese Lunar New Year is called "Tet," and it is the most important holiday in Vietnam.
14. Vietnam is the largest producer of black pepper in the world.

15. Vietnam has over 3,000 kilometres of underground tunnels that were used by the Viet Cong during the Vietnam War.
16. The Vietnamese are the fifth-largest seafood consumers in the world.
17. The Vietnamese love to eat Pho, a traditional noodle soup made with beef or chicken.
18. Vietnam is home to over 50 different ethnic groups.
19. The Vietnamese people believe that their ancestors' spirits play a role in their daily lives and make offerings to them regularly.
20. Vietnam's flag has a bright red background with a yellow star in the centre, representing the communist government.

Printed in Great Britain
by Amazon